making disciples

confirmand's journal

William H. Willimon

Confirmand's Journal for Making Disciples: Confirmation Through Mentoring
A Mentoring Program by William H. Willimon

With gratitude to Mark Flynn who was a contributor to the original edition.

This Confirmand's Journal is accompanied by a Mentor's Guide and a Coordinator's Guide.

Scripture quotations are from the New Revised Standard Version Bible, copyright © 1989 National Council of the Churches of Christ in the United States of America. Used by permission. All rights reserved worldwide. http://nrsvbibles.org/

English translations of The Nicene Creed © 1988 English Language Liturgical Consultation (ELLC). www.englishtexts.org. Used by permission.

Editor: Jack Radcliffe
Designer: Ken Strickland

Websites are constantly changing. Although the websites recommended in this resource were checked at the time this unit was developed, we recommend that you double-check all sites to verify that they are still live and that they are still suitable for students before doing an activity.

ISBN: 9781501848209
PACP10519408-01

18 19 20 21 22 23 24 25 26 27 — 10 9 8 7 6 5 4 3 2 1

MANUFACTURED IN THE UNITED STATES OF AMERICA

Contents

Welcome to Making Disciples!

You are beginning an adventure, a journey—confirmation—that will lead you into deeper faith and a more active commitment to Christian discipleship. In school, you have probably studied a variety of subjects that required you to read books, memorize facts and figures, and think in new ways.

Growing in your discipleship requires a different kind of learning. Never did Jesus say, "Think about me," or "Consider these ideas about me." Rather, what he said to those he met was, "Follow me!"

Probably, this is not the first time you have thought about the Christian faith. In one way or another Jesus has met you, perhaps even when you were unaware that it was Jesus. You don't know everything about Jesus, but you know enough to be curious, to want to deepen your understanding of his way, and to be better equipped to follow Jesus. That's what this process of confirmation will help you to do.

Most of the Gospels begin with Jesus walking along some road, seeing people engaged in everyday activity, and calling out to them, "Follow me!" Surely the people had questions like, "Who are you?" or "Where are you going?" or "What does this mean for my life?"

Those questions were not answered at first. Rather, their questions about Jesus were answered along the way, after these first disciples walked away from what they were doing and stumbled after Jesus. If they were going to learn more about Jesus, they first had to follow Jesus, to walk with him and listen to him as he explained himself. As their journey unfolded, Jesus taught them and revealed truths to them that gradually resulted in a greater commitment to him.

MAKING DISCIPLES assumes that the best way to grow in your discipleship, to deepen in your Christian faith, and to better understand how Jesus wants to enlist you in his work is along the way as you are actively trying to keep up with Jesus. So, you will find that MAKING DISCIPLES guides you through a series of activities that are designed to challenge you to expand your understanding and to deepen your commitment to the God who is committed to you, the Savior who has called you to participate in his salvation of the world.

An important part of your confirmation journey is this Confiirmand's Journal. Your journal provides a place where you can describe highlights, memories, and details of your journey. A journal is something like a diary where you record what you are thinking, learning, and doing along the way.

In MAKING DISCIPLES, your journal asks questions that cause you to think and answer in new ways. There are also suggested activities that enable you to grow in your experience of discipleship.

MAKING DISCIPLES consists of thirteen sessions. You will experience each of the sessions with an adult guide whom we will call a mentor. Your mentor will do the same things you do throughout this process and will share his or her thoughts with you about those experiences, just as you will share yours. You and your mentor are meant to be a team.

You can't think up the Christian faith on your own or discover the call of Christ by yourself. Every Christian must be told the story of Jesus, must receive the faith as a gift from the hands of others, and grow in commitment to the faith by looking over the shoulders of more experienced Christians. That's why this confirmation program pairs you with a mentor, a guide who will work with you through the activities in MAKING DISCIPLES.

Your church and pastor have chosen possible mentors who have special gifts for helping develop Christians. Once you are paired with a mentor, the two of you will regularly meet together. At the end of each session with your mentor, you will look ahead and plan a time for your next meeting and decide on themes you will engage.

MAKING DISCIPLES is a flexible process that you and your mentor can adapt to your individual schedules, needs, questions, and sense of calling. Jesus Christ has called you to follow him. You have begun this walk of faith and service; MAKING DISCIPLES is designed to give you encouragement along the way!

— Will Willimon

Session 1: Getting Acquainted

In this first session, you will become acquainted with your mentor. Relax, be yourself, and get to know each other as you begin this journey of faith together.

Mentor/Student Time

1. A good way to get to know someone is to ask questions. Tell about yourself and your experiences as a way of inviting the other person to be open with you. Use the space provided to record some information about your partner.

    • Tell me about your family.

    • What was it like growing up in church?

    • What are some of your best memories of church?

    • What is a sad memory about church or family?

    • What is/was school like for you?

    • What is one of the best things about your life today?

    • What are your hopes for the future?

2. Find out something about each other's faith experience and take notes on responses.

    • Have you always been a churchgoer?

    • What is important to you about being a part of this church?

    • When did you first know you were a Christian?

3. Talk about your expectations for this confirmation process.

   • What do you hope will happen during this time? Are you excited or nervous?

   • What are you worried about regarding this process?

   • What is one question about the Christian faith, the church, or the Bible that you hope to have answered during our time together?

4. Together, choose a time when you will pray for each other. Use the pictures you have exchanged to help you remember.

5. Bring your Bible to church each Sunday during the confirmation process. When Scripture is read during worship, look up the passage and follow along in your Bible. List any questions you have about these passages and note your observations.

Close your time together by saying individual short prayers asking God to be with you in this confirmation process and thanking God for your partner.

Your Luke Journal

Have you ever kept a journal? A journal is a place to record one's experiences while on a journey. Think, for example, of the world's great explorers and their writings. Without a record of their journeys, important details and discoveries of their trips would have been lost or forgotten. The same thing is true for you.

A Christian reads, ponders, and is shaped by Scripture. Throughout the coming weeks as you meet together, you will read the entire Gospel of Luke. Together, decide what your reading schedule will be (for example, one chapter every day) so that both of you are reading at the same pace.

As you read each chapter, record your comments, reactions, and questions in "Your Luke Journal" on pages 44-48. Then, take time at the beginning of each session to check in with each other and talk about your ideas. Discussion of your journal entries is a great way to have meaningful conversations with each other.

Session 2: God

This session helps you look at one of the three persons of the Trinity: God the Creator. Father may be our most familiar image of God. In the following sessions, you will have an opportunity to explore this and other names of God as mentor and confirmand study theology together.

Mentor/Student Time

1. Check in with each other to see how the reading of the Gospel of Luke is progressing. Review your notes in "Your Luke Journal" (pages 44-48). If either of you has questions, talk about them. What is your biggest challenge in reading Luke's witness to Jesus? If necessary, consult a Bible dictionary or commentary for help in answering some of your questions. However, it isn't necessary to answer all questions. You may address some and agree to think about others, or you may ask for assistance from another mentor pairing or your pastor. Talk about whether you are comfortable with the reading pace you have established and make adjustments if necessary.

2. Draw a picture or symbol depicting your earliest memory of God.

3. Draw something to show how you imagine God to be now.

4. Look at the two drawings or symbols. What do they represent? How are they different? How has your understanding of God changed over the years?

5. A creed is a brief, traditional, widely affirmed statement of our faith. Read the following creeds together. You will note that these creeds have a Trinitarian form, moving from a statement of faith, "I believe in God," to affirmations about God the Father, God the Son, and God the Holy Spirit. The creeds will guide us in our theological reflection upon God. Circle the words or phrases in the creeds that you find interesting.

From the Apostles' Creed (Traditional Version)

I believe in God the Father Almighty,
maker of heaven and earth.

From the Nicene Creed

We believe in one God,
the Father, the Almighty,
maker of heaven and earth,
of all that is, seen and unseen.

6. Which of the references to God in the creeds do you find most relevant to your life at this time? Why?

7. Name any new ideas about God that are reflected in these creeds.

8. When have you felt that God was with you in a particularly real and vivid way? Have you ever felt like God has left you alone? Talk about when and where that feeling occurred in your life.

9. Together, read aloud Psalm 33. List the words or phrases that describe God or God's actions. According to this writer, what is God like? Do you see God in this way? Why, or why not? Is there any one word or phrase that stands out as you read and reflect? Use the space at the top of the next page also.

10. Together, read aloud Genesis 1:27-31. According to this Scripture, we are created in the image of God. What do you think it means to be created in the image of God?

Close your session with prayer, using some of the images of God you have talked about during this session. Thank God for this time together, and ask God's blessing for each other in the coming week.

Conclude by praying together the Lord's Prayer. This is the prayer Jesus gave his disciples when they said, "Lord, teach us to pray." Choose one of the following versions.

Our Father, who art in heaven,
> **hallowed be thy name.**
> **Thy kingdom come,**
> **thy will be done on earth as it is in heaven.**
Give us this day our daily bread.
And forgive us our trespasses,
> **as we forgive those who trespass against us.**
And lead us not into temptation,
> **but deliver us from evil.**
For thine is the kingdom, and the power, and the glory,
> **forever. Amen.**
(From the Ritual of the Former Methodist Church)

Our Father, who art in heaven,
> **hallowed be thy name;**
> **thy kingdom come,**
> **thy will be done, on earth as it is in heaven.**
Give us this day our daily bread;
and forgive us our debts,
> **as we forgive our debtors;**
and lead us not into temptation,
> **but deliver us from evil.**
For thine is the kingdom and the power, and the glory,
> **forever. Amen.**
(From the Ritual of the Former Evangelical United Brethren Church)

Session 3: Jesus

This session guides you in sharing what you believe about Jesus, the second person of the Trinity. It also explores the presence of Jesus in worship, especially in the Service of the Lord's Supper (Eucharist or Holy Communion). You and your mentor will attend a Communion service together as part of this session.

Mentor/Student Time

1. How is your reading of Luke's Gospel going? Take a look at "Your Luke Journal" on pages 44-48. What have you learned about Jesus from reading the Gospel of Luke? Make notes below. If either of you has questions, take time to share them.

2. Together, read aloud what each of the following creeds says about Jesus. Circle the words or phrases that stand out in your mind as interesting, unusual, or unclear. Note the things Jesus did or said that are mentioned in the creeds. Compare what you have learned about Jesus from reading Luke's Gospel with what is said (or not said!) in the creeds.

From the Apostles' Creed (Traditional Version)

And in Jesus Christ his only Son our Lord:
> **who was conceived by the Holy Spirit,**
>> **born of the Virgin Mary,**
>> **suffered under Pontius Pilate,**
>> **was crucified, dead, and buried;***
> **the third day he rose from the dead;**
> **he ascended into heaven,**
>> **and sitteth at the right hand of God the Father Almighty;**
> **from thence he shall come to judge the quick and the dead.**

From the Nicene Creed

We believe in one Lord, Jesus Christ,
> **the only Son of God,**
> **eternally begotten of the Father,**
> **God from God, Light from Light,**
> **true God from true God,**
> **begotten, not made,**
> **of one Being with the Father;**
> **through him all things were made.**

For us and for our salvation
> **he came down from heaven,**
> **was incarnate of the Holy Spirit and the Virgin Mary**
> **and became truly human.**

For our sake he was crucified under Pontius Pilate;
>   **he suffered death and was buried.**
>   **On the third day he rose again**
>   **in accordance with the Scriptures;**
>   **he ascended into heaven**
>   **and is seated at the right hand of the Father.**
>   **He will come again in glory**
>   **to judge the living and the dead,**
>   **and his kingdom will have no end.**

* Traditional use of this creed includes these words: "He descended into hell."

** universal

3. For exactly one minute, list every word you can think of to describe Christ.

4. As one of you reads aloud Philippians 2:1-11, the other should list the words Paul used to describe Jesus.

5. Attend a service where Holy Communion is being celebrated. What images of Christ were incorporated in the service? Where did you notice these images (hymns, symbolic actions, objects in the church, sermon, and so on)?

6. Talk about the Communion service you attended. How did the service focus on Christ? What was your favorite part of the service?

7. Look over the worship guide from the Communion service you attended and note some of the parts in the service that addressed the following topics:

God's goodness

Christ's Sacrifice

Christ's work in cross and resurrection

Sin and forgiveness

God's Grace

Christ's presence with us

8. John 3:16 is a well-known Bible verse. Why do you think so many people know this verse? What does the verse mean to you?

Close your session with prayer, using some of the images of Jesus that you have talked about in this session. Thank God for this time together, and ask God's blessing for each other in the coming week. Expect Jesus to show up in your lives in the days ahead, even as he appeared to people as recorded in Luke's Gospel. Conclude by praying the Lord's Prayer together.

Session 4: Holy Spirit

Mentor/Student Time

The Holy Spirit is God in action—God becoming present to us in power and love. In this session, you will have the opportunity to learn more about the Holy Spirit, the third person of the Trinity.

1. Luke's Gospel constantly emphasizes the work of the Holy Spirit (such as Luke's account of Jesus' birth, Luke 1:35; Jesus' baptism, Luke 3:21-22; and Jesus' sermon in Nazareth, Luke 4:14-28). What have you learned about the Holy Spirit from your reading of Luke? If either of you has questions, particularly about the work of the Holy Spirit as described in Luke's Gospel, take time to talk about them.

2. Together, read the story of the Day of Pentecost from Acts 2:1-21. What images from this story stand out for you?

3. What are some of the physical ways people sensed the presence of the Spirit on that day?

4. How are you aware of the Holy Spirit in the world today? Have you experienced anything you would call "the working of the Holy Spirit"? In many of our churches today we don't hear much about the Holy Spirit. The focus seems to be more upon God the Father or God the Son. Why do you think that is true? What do we lose in our faith when we neglect the Holy Spirit?

5. Read what the creeds tell us about the Holy Spirit. Circle any words or phrases that you find interesting, unusual, or confusing.

From the Apostles' Creed (Traditional Version)

I believe in the Holy Spirit,
   the holy catholic** church,
   the communion of saints,
   the forgiveness of sins,
   the resurrection of the body,
   and the life everlasting. Amen.

From the Nicene Creed

We believe in the Holy Spirit, the Lord, the giver of life,
   who proceeds from the Father and the Son,
   who with the Father and the Son
     is worshiped and glorified,
   who has spoken through the prophets.
We believe in the one holy catholic* and apostolic church.
We acknowledge one baptism
   for the forgiveness of sins.
We look for the resurrection of the dead,
   and the life of the world to come. Amen.

* Traditional use of this creed includes these words: "He descended into hell."
** universal

6. Which creed makes the most sense to you when it talks about the Holy Spirit? Why?

7. Together, read 2 Timothy 1:1-14. In this passage, Paul talks about the role of the Holy Spirit as the presence of Christ working in young Timothy's life. It's important to remember that the Holy Spirit is the Spirit of Christ—Christ doing in us, here and now, what Christ did for his disciples in the Gospel of Luke. What does it mean to you that the Holy Spirit is "living in us"?

8. Make a bookmark displaying one of the symbols commonly used to represent the Holy Spirit, such as a dove, flame, or mighty wind. Exchange bookmarks and keep them in your Bibles as a reminder to pray for each other.

9. Don't worry about what you and your partner don't know about the Holy Spirit. It is the nature of the Holy Spirit to be mysterious and often difficult to define or describe. Rather, talk together about how you experience God's presence and guidance in your daily life—a basic function of the Spirit. Note below any experiences or truths about the Holy Spirit that you want to remember in the days ahead.

Close your session with prayer, mentioning some of the images of the Holy Spirit you have talked about during this session. Ask the Holy Spirit to bless your time together and guide you through the coming week. Conclude by praying the Lord's Prayer together.

Session 5: Worship

Christians are those who come together and worship the God who has come to us in Jesus Christ. In worship, the church gathers and listens as God's Word is read and preached, prays for the needs of the congregation and the world, and praises the God who comes to us in our times of worship and strengthens us for discipleship. As part of this session, you are asked to attend worship together on several occasions in your church, as well as in other churches in your community.

Mentor/Student Time

1. Jesus begins his ministry at a service of worship in his hometown synagogue (Luke 4). Together, read about that service (and what happened after Jesus preached!). Do you see a similar pattern in the way your church worships?

2. Together, read Psalm 95:1-6. What first comes to your mind when you hear the word *worship*? What do you think is the most important part of a worship service? Why?

3. How many parts of the worship service can you remember? Make a list of every act of worship that occurs in your Sunday morning service. Then look at a bulletin to see how well you remembered.

4. The church year is divided into six different seasons: Advent, Christmas, Epiphany, Lent, Easter, and Pentecost. How does your church observe the various seasons (special decorations, music, different colors)? What is your favorite season of the Christian year? What does this season mean to you?

5. In what ways does worship affect your day-to-day life?

6. After you have attended services together in at least two other churches in your community, reflect on those experiences. What are some of the similarities and differences between the worship service in your church and the services you attended in other churches?

7. What are some similarities and differences among the buildings and the symbols that were used in worship?

8. Read John 4:24. What do you think it means to worship in "spirit and truth"?

9. **Optional Activity:** Design and create a banner that uses one or more Christian symbols to illustrate some aspects of Sunday worship. Use the space below to sketch your design and make notes. Ask if you may hang the banner in your church for a few Sundays.

10. **Optional Activity:** Randomly select people to interview as they are leaving worship on Sunday. Ask each of them, "Why do you attend worship at our church?" Compare and discuss the responses you receive. Are there any common themes in their responses? Use the space on this page to record answers and make notes.

Close your session with prayer. Ask God to be with you in worship and to help you experience God's presence. Conclude by praying the Lord's Prayer together.

Session 6: The Bible

In this session, you will explore the Bible as God's persuasive, empowering, and compelling word. Focus on how and where God's Word is at work in your life and in the world.

Mentor/Student Time

1. We sometimes speak of the Bible as "the Word of God." Discuss with each other how, in reading Luke's Gospel, these ancient words have jumped off the page and become God's Word addressed to you in the here and now.

2. Imagine that you have been asked to give a short testimonial (three minutes or less) to your belief in Jesus as the Messiah, the Lord, the Savior of the world. Take a few moments to compose that speech and then share your speech with each other.

3. In the past weeks, you have been introduced to the Gospel of Luke. Find a Bible commentary in your church, local library, or on the Internet. Read an introductory article about the Gospel of Luke. What new discoveries have you made while reading this commentary on Luke? Has learning more about the history, the context, and the themes of Luke's Gospel helped you better appreciate this part of God's Word?

4. There are many different translations and versions of the Bible. Read the parable of the good Samaritan in Luke 10:29-37 (a story found only in Luke's Gospel) in three different Bible versions (such as the New Revised Standard, The Common English Bible, King James, New

International, or Good News Bible). The name of the specific version is usually printed on the cover of the Bible or on its title page. Which version do you like the best? Why?

5. Why do you think there are so many different versions of the Bible?

6. What are some of your favorite Old Testament stories (Creation, Noah, the Exodus, Deborah, David and Goliath, and Jonah)? Together, find and read one or two of these stories. It's important to know how to use a concordance, Bible dictionary, and commentary in order to better understand Scripture.

7. What questions do you have about the Bible? Where do you think you might find the answers to your questions?

8. Why do you think people read the Bible? What makes it difficult for you to read the Bible regularly?

9. Most sermons are based upon some biblical text. Recall some of your pastor's recent sermons. What do you think are some of your pastor's favorite Scripture passages?

As a closing prayer, give thanks to God for revealing God's ways to us in Scripture. Conclude by praying the Lord's Prayer together.

Session 7: Saints and Gifts

Saints are Christians, past and present, who have been enlisted by God to work with God in transforming the world. Saints are not necessarily very religious nor morally perfect people. The Bible calls all baptized believers "saints." You will have the opportunity to talk about and to visit with saints whom you know and to think about how people in every age are called to be saints.

Mentor/Student Time

1. Check in with each other regarding your progress in reading the Gospel of Luke. Look at "Your Luke Journal" on pages 44-48. What have you learned about saints and gifts from your reading of the Gospel? If either of you has questions, take time to talk about them together.

2. What does the word *saint* mean to you? Who are saints?

3. Read Hebrews 11:1–12:1. This passage is often referred to as the "great roll call of saints." These people did some extraordinary things. Where do you think they received the power to endure hardships and to accomplish great things in service to God?

4. List the names of people who have been important in your life of faith. After each name on your list, note how that person influenced your spiritual life and include at least one quality in him or her that you admire.

5. Read 1 Corinthians 1:1-9. Are you a saint? Why, or why not? How does the last part of verse 2 in this passage seem to define a *saint*?

6. Prepare to visit with a saint from your congregation. You might choose someone you know or ask your pastor for a recommendation. It might be someone who is currently active in the congregation or someone who lives in a retirement or nursing home. Do you feel awkward or uncomfortable about making such a visit? Why?

7. Before visiting, compile a list of questions you would like to ask this person that will help you learn more about his or her faith, daily life, and church experience through the years. After your visit, write about or draw something to represent some of the information you learned about the person.

8. Reflect on your visit. Was the visit what you expected? What, if anything, surprised you about the individual you visited? What did you learn from the person's response to your questions regarding the development of his or her Christian faith? What is something you learned from this person that you would like to imitate in your personal faith life?

9. We know that our faith changes over time, just as we change over time. How has your faith changed as a result of participating in this confirmation process? How is your faith different from what it was two years ago, five years ago, or when you were a very small child? Create a timeline of your faith experience using the instructions below.

- Look at the timeline on the next page. The top line is the date line. At the far left, write your date of birth. At the far right, write the current date. In between, with vertical strokes, divide the line into equal parts, such as every 3, 5, or 10 years, and write the year above every mark.
- The bottom line is the place line. Under it write the names of the places where you lived at the points along your timeline.
- In the space above the top line and related to dates, write in words or phrases that represent significant national and world events that you remember or were part of your life.
- Between the two lines write specific milestone events in your life.
- Below the bottom line add details that come to mind, keeping them in proper reference to the date line. Include notes on the following three categories:
  a. Personal experiences and remembrances, such as family trips, honors, or memorable moments
  b. Names of people who were important to you, with whom you spent time, saints who influenced you in positive ways, and people you remember now with fondness
  c. Events that helped shape your faith, such as church camp, death of someone you loved, high points and low points alike
- Share the timeline of your faith journey with your partner and talk together about what you learn about the nature of faith by looking at your timelines.

10. How can saints, those with us now and great Christians of the past, encourage us in our faith?

Close your session with prayer. In your prayer, say aloud the names of saints whom you have known, name one gift God has given you for which you are grateful, and ask God for a gift that will strengthen you in your witness to others as a saint. Conclude by praying the Lord's Prayer together.

Faith Timeline

Date Line: _____

Place Line: _____

Session 8: Ministry

This session emphasizes two important points. First, just as we all are saints, we all are called to be ministers, servants of God, and servants to others. Second, ministry happens in a wide variety of settings—some inside the church and some outside. This session will give you an opportunity to experience these two dimensions of ministry.

Mentor/Student Time

1. Look back at "Your Luke Journal" on pages 44-48. As you have read through the Gospel of Luke, can you think of a time when Jesus was a minister to others? Can you recall any instance when someone ministered to Jesus? Do you think that one purpose of Luke's Gospel is to strengthen Jesus' followers in their ministry?

2. Read Matthew 25:31-46. What do you think Jesus was saying about ministry in these verses? What words or phrases impress you in this passage?

3. Read Luke 10:1-23. Jesus sent out seventy-two others to help him in his ministry and to do some of the same things he did in ministry. In what ways does Jesus send forth people in your church today that are similar to ways Jesus sent out people in Luke 10?

4. List three ways your church ministers to its members.

5. List three ways your church ministers to those in your community.

6. List three ways your church has ministered to you.

7. Obtain a copy of your church's Service of Baptism. (Most churches include this service in their hymnals.) What does it mean to say that, in baptism, every Christian becomes a minister? List ways you minister to others.

8. Do you see a need among members in your congregation or in your community? Is God calling you to step up and help meet this need in ministry? How can you do so?

9. List below some community ministries your church supports or participates in (for example, soup kitchens, shelters, Meals on Wheels, food pantry, clothing distribution, and so on)? Choose one ministry in which you will work together at least twice during the remaining time of your confirmation experience.

   • We will minister by: _____

10. After your first volunteer experience, reflect on how it felt to minister in this particular situation. Answer the following: Was your experience what you expected? What surprised you about the experience? What was the most memorable part of the experience? Would you do this again? What new things did you learn about ministry? How did the people you served react to your ministry?

Close your session with prayer, giving thanks for those who have ministered to you and also asking God to bless you in your ministry to others. Conclude by praying the Lord's Prayer together.

Session 9: Baptism

This session is about baptism and emphasizes the truth that confirmation is an extension of the baptismal promises—not a replacement of them or an additional requirement for membership in the family of faith. Baptism is the sign that designates a Christian, the gift of God whereby we receive what we need to be faithful disciples of Christ.

Mentor/Student Time

1. In your reading of Luke, did you note that Jesus' ministry begins with his baptism (Luke 3:21-22)? Our ministry also begins in our baptism. Note and discuss any questions raised by Luke's account of Jesus' baptism or any questions that have arisen while reading Luke's Gospel.

2. Where and when were you baptized? Do you have any special mementos of the day? What happened? Do you have baptismal sponsors or godparents? Share baptismal memories and mementos with each other.

3. If either of you has not been baptized, how has this confirmation process served as preparation for your eventual baptism? Your pastor can provide information about your church's baptismal practices and help you to decide whether this is a good time for you to be baptized.

4. Discuss the Service of Baptism as it is practiced in your congregation. Look at the service order in your worship book or hymnal if you need help. Make note of any questions you have.

5. Read the account of Jesus' baptism found in Matthew 3:1-17. What happened in Jesus' baptism? How is this version the same as or different from the account in Luke 3:1-22? How is it the same as or different from your personal baptism? If a dove descended and a voice from heaven spoke at your baptism, what would you hope the voice would say?

6. Just as a dove, symbolizing the descent of the Holy Spirit, rested upon Jesus at his baptism, so we are given the gift of the Holy Spirit at our baptism, an act that is symbolized by the laying on of hands. The Holy Spirit and its gifts are essential for faithful Christian discipleship. How have you felt the Holy Spirit empowering and strengthening you in your daily walk with Christ?

7. Together, attend a service of baptism. Then discuss the following statement: Confirmation is a rite that symbolizes the confirmation of baptism, particularly the gifts of the Holy Spirit. Write a few sentences in response to each of these questions: "Why do Christians baptize?" and "What is the meaning of confirmation?"

8. The church has traditionally referred to baptism a "sacrament." Sacraments are gifts of God to us, whereby God uses the stuff of everyday life to speak to us, to minister to us, and to be present to us. What are some of the gifts God gives us through the gift of baptism? What are some of the promises God makes in baptism? What are the promises made to God by those who are baptized?

9. The following Scripture passages talk about baptism. As time allows, read them together. Then describe the meaning of each passage using your own words.

   • Colossians 2:12: _____

   • Acts 2:17: _____

   • Galatians 4:4-7: _____

   • Matthew 28:18-20: _____

   • Mark 1:9-11: _____

   • Ephesians 2:8-9: _____

10. Design and create a banner depicting one or more of the meanings of baptism you have discussed. This banner could be for yourself, for your church sanctuary, or a gift to the next person baptized in your congregation. Talk with your pastor for help in coordinating the project if you wish to give away your banner. Use the space below to plan and sketch the design for your banner.

Close the session with prayer, thanking God for the gift of baptism. Conclude by praying the Lord's Prayer together.

Session 10: Spiritual Life

The regular practice of spiritual disciplines such as prayer, meditation, and Bible study is crucial to the life of faith. In this session, you will discuss these practices and share some prayer experiences together.

Mentor/student time

1. Look at "Your Luke Journal" on pages 44-48. Can you recall instances of prayer that occur in Luke's Gospel? What have you learned about prayer from your reading of Luke? It is customary on Sunday mornings, prior to the reading of Scripture in worship, to have a Prayer for Illumination, a prayer that asks for the gift of the Holy Spirit to guide us in our reading and hearing of Scripture. Why do you think it is important to pray before reading Scripture?

2. When you are together, talk about how it feels to pray. What would make it easier or more comfortable for you to pray? Prayer involves both speaking to and listening to God. Which do you find to be a greater challenge in prayer: speaking or listening?

3. Read Matthew 6:9-13. Which words or phrases in this passage are most interesting to you? In your own words, restate the message of this passage. How does this Scripture apply to your personal spiritual experiences?

4. What do you think it means to pray, "Your kingdom come"? What does the kingdom of God look like? Describe, write, or sketch something here to represent the kingdom of God.

5. Prayer is when we bring our needs before God and ask God to do for us that which we are unable to do for ourselves. Sometimes our prayers are limited to the needs of ourselves, our families, or our church. How might we discipline ourselves to broaden the scope of our prayers to include the needs of those who are not near to us?

   • Make a list of world issues that you will include in your prayer time during the coming weeks.

   • Record here the prayer that you wrote earlier together and that may be offered to your pastor for possible use in a worship service of your church.

6. In addition to prayer, other practices of the spiritual life include meditation, sabbath keeping, Bible study, fasting, regular worship attendance, and service to those in need. What is a spiritual practice that you want to learn more about and perhaps add to your spiritual walk. Together, search for more information about this practice (checking the Internet, asking your pastor, or working with another team). Make notes in the space below.

7. How can these practices affect daily living? How might daily prayer affect your attitude toward the events of the day? How might Bible study affect your prayer life and life in general?

8. Is it difficult for you to maintain the practice of daily prayer? If so, why? What changes can you make in order to include daily prayer and the practice of other spiritual disciplines as a regular part of your life?

9. Do you believe that prayer can actually change things in your life and in the world? Give an example of something you hope could be changed through prayer.

Close this session by thanking God for the gift of prayer. Conclude by praying either the traditional version of the Lord's Prayer or by praying the prayer you recorded on page 32.

Your Prayer Journal

Have you enjoyed keeping a journal while reading Luke's Gospel? In the days ahead, keep a prayer journal using pages 49-54. Briefly write about people, needs, and situations for which you are praying. Beside each petition, record when you believe you have received answers to that prayer. Look back to your prayer journal over the coming months. Be patient and persistent as you wait for answers and guidance.

Session 11: Death and Resurrection

Our faith in Christ speaks clearly to the issues of death and resurrection. In this session, you will discuss both our hope in Christ and our support of one another in times of death and grief.

Mentor/Student Time

1. As you have read Luke's Gospel, what have you learned about death and resurrection? Take time to share questions and observations.

2. Locate a copy of your church's funeral service. Can you tell from the service what your church believes about death and resurrection? Summarize those beliefs in one or two sentences or paragraphs.

3. Read John 11:1-44; 1 Corinthians 15:51-57; and 2 Corinthians 4:7-14. What emotions do people experience when someone they love has died? How might these emotions be expressed during a funeral service? What stands out to you in each passage?

4. Share ideas about the sort of funeral service you would want.

   • Music:

   • Bible passages:

   • Mood:

   • People you hope would attend:

5. Together, if possible, attend a funeral service. What, if anything, surprised you about the service? What emotions did you observe in others? What emotions did you experience? Did anything happen that you didn't understand? Why do you think we have funerals instead of simply burying or cremating the people who die? Why do we have a public gathering? In what way did attending this service help to prepare you for your personal encounters with mourning and loss? Use the space below to reflect.

6. What do you think should be the focus of a funeral service?

7. In one minute, write as many words as you can think of to describe eternal life and heaven.

8. Recall a funeral you have attended for a friend or family member. What stands out in your memory of this experience?

Choose a prayer from your church's Service of Death and Resurrection to close this session. Or, close with prayer, giving thanks for God's presence in times of sorrow and for God's gift of peace. Conclude by praying the Lord's Prayer together. Note the concluding "forever" in the Lord's Prayer as a closing affirmation of our faith in God's gift of eternal life.

Session 12: Life in the Church

The church is sometimes called "the body of Christ." The church is the primary visible, bodily way that Christ is present in the world. Being the body of Christ means that the church must deal with practical, organizational, and institutional issues of function and form. In this session, you will discuss what makes your church work and talk about your involvement in Christ's body on earth at this time and place.

Mentor/Student Time

1. Luke depicts Jesus as beginning his ministry by calling a group of disciples. Whatever Jesus wanted to do in the world, he chose not to do it alone. He gathered a group of followers who worked together sharing Christ's ministry in the world. How have you seen that group at work as you read in Luke's Gospel? What have you learned about community life and individual gifts from your reading of Luke?

2. Read Ephesians 4:1-6. What do we share as Christians in this congregation? What gifts has Christ given to us as we join together?

3. Read Romans 12:5-8. The church often calls itself "the body of Christ." In what ways do you see the members of the congregation working together to accomplish God's work? Which part of the body do you think you are? How might you become a more active part of the body?

4. Why do you think people join a church? What are the good things about being a church member?

5. Think about the church as a body. List on and around the outline below the names of members or organizations of the church that carry out particular parts of the body's work. For example, the evangelism committee may be both legs and mouth; the food pantry may be the loving heart.

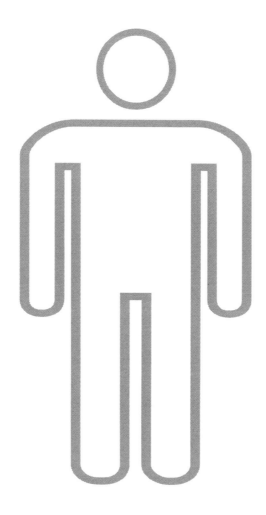

6. Do you think your church body works well? Is it well-coordinated? Do the parts work well together?

7. Attend a church board meeting together and take notes about what happens there. How was this meeting different from other organizational meetings? How was it the same? What was most interesting about the meeting? What business took up the greatest portion of the time? What was the main goal of the meeting? In your opinion, did the group operate like the body of Christ?

8. On which church committee would you like to serve? Why?

9. Review a copy of your church's current budget. Which items on the budget are the most expensive? What does the budget tell you about the church's priorities? Were you surprised by any information in the budget?

10. Design a poster or bulletin board that highlights one facet of human need that your congregation is trying to address with budgeted funds. Use the space below to plan and sketch your banner. Ask for permission to hang the poster in some public area.

11. How would you respond to someone making this statement: "I think a person can be a good Christian without being part of a church." Talk about responses.

12. In one minute, list all the good things your church does for people inside and outside of the church.

Close this session with prayer, giving thanks for God's gift of the church. Ask God to guide your church in service to others. Conclude by praying the Lord's Prayer together.

Session 13: The Faith Journey Continues

Confirmation is not the end of the faith journey. It certainly is not a "graduation" out of the church! Confirmation is a door into the future, a time to gain the equipment and skills needed to continue with confidence the journey of discipleship that begins in baptism.

Mentor/Student Time

1. By now you should have concluded your reading of Luke's Gospel. What is an important learning you received from your Bible reading? What is one question that sticks in your mind that you would like to explore in future reading of Scripture?

2. Read Romans 8:31-39. In these verses, Paul testifies to the hope for constant communion with Christ that gives us endurance. How does being a follower of Christ give you hope? In your past, what aspects of life have hindered you from having a better relationship with Jesus Christ?

3. List some of the ways your church provides opportunity for people to grow in their faith. Put a check mark beside those opportunities in which you have previously participated. Put a star beside activities and events that you hope to take advantage of in the future.

4. List some ways you can help other people in the church to grow or experience God's hope for the future (for example, teaching Sunday school, visiting homebound members, providing childcare for church meetings, helping to set up for church activities). Then select one of these opportunities and commit to participation.

• I choose: _____

5. Have you ever helped someone to grow in the faith and to find hope during a sad or hopeless time? Share what you said and did that ministered to another person.

6. Using a Bible concordance or Internet resources, look up the word *disciple*. Then browse the Gospel of Luke and note some of the interactions between Jesus and his disciples. What does being a Christian disciple mean to you? How does it aid you in your discipleship and in becoming a faithful member of the church?

7. During this confirmation process, how have you seen yourself grow in understanding of God? How would you characterize your relationship with God at this point in your life?

8.   As you live into the future, what is one spiritual practice you might engage that could contribute to your growth as a disciple?

As you conclude the session, exchange books with your mentor. On page 57 in the Mentor's Guide is a place to record confirmation memories. Also on the page is a section titled "A Prayer of Blessing for My Mentor" from the confirmand. In the space provided, write a brief prayer of blessing for your mentor, thanking God for the faith journey you have shared and for all that is to come.

On the following page in this book, the Confirmand's Journal, is a place for your mentor to write a brief prayer of blessing for you. Once you and your mentor have finished writing the prayers of blessing, swap books again so that you have your Confirmand Journal with the prayer from your mentor. Conclude by praying the Lord's Prayer together.

Confirmation Memories

Mentored by: _____

Confirmed on: _____

By: _____

(Minister/Pastor)

At _____

(Church)

Sponsors:

_____

_____

_____

Favorite Memories of the Service:

Music from the Service:

A Treasured Bible Passage:

A Prayer of Blessing for My Confirmand from the Mentor:

Signed: _____

(the Mentor)

Your Luke Journal

Chapter 1

_____

_____

_____

_____

Chapter 2

_____

_____

_____

_____

Chapter 3

_____

_____

_____

_____

Chapter 4

_____

_____

_____

_____

Chapter 5

_____

_____

_____

Chapter 6

_____

_____

_____

Chapter 7

_____

_____

_____

Chapter 8

_____

_____

_____

Chapter 9

_____

_____

_____

Chapter 10

_____

_____

_____

Chapter 11

_____

_____

_____

Chapter 12

_____

_____

_____

Chapter 13

_____

_____

_____

Chapter 14

_____

_____

_____

_____

Chapter 15

_____

_____

_____

Chapter 16

_____

_____

_____

Chapter 17

_____

_____

_____

Chapter 18

_____

_____

_____

Chapter 19

_____

_____

_____

_____

Chapter 20

_____

_____

_____

Chapter 21

_____

_____

_____

Chapter 22

_____

_____

_____

Chapter 23

_____

_____

_____

Chapter 24

_____

_____

_____

Your Prayer Journal

In the following pages, write about things for which you are praying. Beside each petition, record when you believe you receive answers to specific prayers. Look back at your prayer journal over the coming months. Be patient and persistent as you wait for answers and guidance.

Prayers

Answers

Prayers	Answers

Prayers	Answers

Prayers   Answers

_____   _____

_____   _____

_____   _____

_____   _____

_____   _____

_____   _____

_____   _____

_____   _____

_____   _____

_____   _____

_____   _____

_____   _____

_____   _____

_____   _____

_____   _____

_____   _____

Prayers	Answers

Prayers   Answers

_____   _____

_____   _____

_____   _____

_____   _____

_____   _____

_____   _____

_____   _____

_____   _____

_____   _____

_____   _____

_____   _____

_____   _____

_____   _____

_____   _____

_____   _____

_____   _____

_____   _____

Made in United States
Orlando, FL
17 April 2022